D0580457

What

Nature

Editors-in-Chief Deborah Chasman, Joshua Cohen

Managing Editor Adam McGee

Senior Editor Chloe Fox

Web and Production Editor Avni Majithia-Sejpal

Poetry Editors Timothy Donnelly, BK Fischer, Stefania Heim

Fiction Editor Junot Díaz

Editorial Assistants Carmen X. Barsomian-Dietrich, Ben Kesslen

Poetry Readers Michelle Dominique Burk, Janet Duffy, Jeff Hipsher, Christopher Janigian, Julie Kantor, Sara Joy Marquez, Lynn Melnick, Diana Khoi Nguyen, Nathan Osorio, Emilie Yardley-Hodges

Publisher Louisa Daniels Kearney

Marketing Manager Anne Boylan

Marketing Associate Michelle Betters

Finance Manager Anthony DeMusis III

Book Distributor The MIT Press, Cambridge, Massachusetts, and London, England

Magazine Distributor Disticor Magazine Distribution Services 800-668-7724, info@disticor.com

Printer Sheridan PA

Board of Advisors Derek Schrier (chairman), Archon Fung, Deborah Fung, Richard M. Locke, Jeff Mayersohn, Jennifer Moses, Scott Nielsen, Martha C. Nussbaum, Robert Pollin, Rob Reich, Hiram Samel, Kim Malone Scott

Cover and Graphic Design Zak Jensen

Typefaces Druk and Adobe Pro Caslon

What Nature is *Boston Review* Forum 6 (43.2)

To become a member or subscribe, visit: bostonreview.net/membership/

For questions about book sales or publicity, contact: Michelle Betters, michelle@bostonreview.net

For questions about subscriptions, call 877-406-2443 or email Customer_Service@BostonReview.info.

Boston Review
PO Box 425786, Cambridge, MA 02142
617-324-1360

ISSN: 0734-2306 / ISBN: 978-1-946511-05-8

Authors retain copyright of their own work.
© 2018, Boston Critic, Inc.

CONTENTS

Editors' Note

Timothy Donnelly, BK Fischer, & Stefania Heim

The poems collected in *What Nature* were written in the predawn of the Sixth Extinction Event. They were written as sea levels rose over a tenth of an inch a year. They were written as albatross on the Midway Atoll fed their young with plastic bottle caps and cigarette lighters mistaken for brightly colored squid. They were written as insect excretions collected from Thai forests formed the shellac that gives jellybeans their sheen. They were not written on Walden Pond or in the Vale of Chamouni. They were not written because poetry can save the Earth. They were written because titanium dioxide is used to whiten ranch dressing and to protect the skin from UV radiation intensified by the depletion of ozone in the stratosphere. They were written in the wake of Katrina, Sandy, Harvey, Irma, and Maria. They were written when Monsanto's website offered "an additional $6 more per acre in cash when [farmers] apply XtendiMax® herbicide with VaporGrip® Technology, now a restricted use pesticide, to their Roundup Ready 2 Xtend soybeans along with endorsed herbicides from Roundup Ready PLUS® Crop Management Solutions." They were written in the months leading up to New York City's announcement that it is seeking billions in damages from BP, Chevron, ConocoPhillips, ExxonMobil, and Royal Dutch Shell for having "deliberately engaged in a campaign of deception and denial about global warming and its impacts." They were written under Trump. If they are a far cry from last century's nature poetry, it is because what "nature" is today is a far cry from sanctuary or retreat or any supposedly tranquil, separate sphere where contemplation might unfold in ease. These poems are not at ease and there is no place left to retreat. They are themselves far cries: urgent calls for rethinking our place on an imperiled planet.

Dennis James Sweeney, "*Leucolepis acanthoneuron*: 'A Freed but Scarred City Tests Trump,' *New York Times*, July 2, 2017, Sunday Edition."

Somewhere in the forest is a clearing.
Somewhere in the clearing is a man.
Somewhere in the man is a spark.
The spark creates worlds, and
leaves them in ruin.

*—Gyrðir Elíasson, "Primary Text," translated
from the Icelandic by Meg Matich*

Silenic Landscape

Alissa Valles

I write you
from the small patch
of this country
that's not on fire

They're all
on the move
carrying bottles
bags

The red needles
fall on rock in patterns
that are prophetic
it's thought

although their reader
has not yet come forward
perhaps not yet
been born

A landscape in which
love
led to slaughter
returns in the shape

of a rock
or a cloud
or a foal
asleep on its side

If I leave this place
now
you'll never
find me

The Human Race

Kathy Nilsson

It won't be long before earth leaves you
Before you move your skeleton around in a wheelbarrow
Like a Venetian chandelier.
Heat from your hands can't keep the lights on.
Your animals end up living inside you.
You empty pinch bottles
And collapse tiny clipper ships onto papier-mâché seas
Ignoring the low screech coming billions of miles towards you.
Your last thoughts settle down like fleas
In bedrooms made from whole cloth in the annals of orchids.

The Embarrassment of Being in the World

Kathy Nilsson

Families of American trees move west
In search of familiar weather.
The sun is putting some of us to death.
News has the repetition of fine needlepoint—
A pair goes out for a stroll but only a man returns
With sense that appeared first in a worm
We declare you unsuitable to be where you are
Police shoot young black man showing a sign
Of young black manhood
Like the woman after the war who didn't remember
Whether their targets were animals or human
I don't recall being American, or even here.

From *Variations on Adonis*

Jesús Castillo

Whatever fashioned us, its fashioning was nothing
      but a woken leaf, shaken
by having only this much time to watch itself dissolve.

Centuries of us became paper to be burned in the houses
of presidents and clerks.

And still we led everyday lives through the waste
       and slaughter.
Just today, for example, I am riding a southbound train,
drinking beer and watching the coastline glitter by.

The mountains seldom speak
but they spoke thus: "We hold the future shape
      of the world of any walking race that can survive.

The crust of the human will crumple in its casket,
      give way to dust and light."

    My veins pulse, hopeful.

And the women work to wake each other up
            in the midst of history swiveling.

When the machines do the lifting, the horizon changes.
How will we destroy each other now?

The women hoist the day up from the well, braid their expenses,
singing: "God is the rotting plants that feed the june bugs,
the order and disorder of the world
            and we are its hands."

And they asked the sky: "Is this world fodder
            or a seed?"
And they unsewed the sky.
And from the punctures in the air
[   ]

God plays in the eternity of childhood as God plays
in the light that washes the days.
The war machines sigh with spent bodies
and the future is a ghost we must embody,
make alive.
Screens paint illusions that loss
snips, and still the masses insist
on sleep without dreams.

In a city of synthetic moods
the children fight sleeplessness with greed,
uproot dream's veins and change the air of waking.

Let sky and earth and man trade limbs.
God plays in the equation.

"There should still be glowworms."

Fresh Kills

Claire Hero

Fresh Kills Landfill in New York, open 1947–2001, was once the largest
landfill in the world, and visible from space.

Our kingdom is of trash

Trash the crown
of gulls wheeling on the methane updrafts

Trash the throne,
this scaffold of carcass and crust

Out of alley and attic, out of sewer and sluice,
trash creeps among us—

Trash the claw, the moving in darkness

Trash the animal out of place:
the body blown against the fence, the meat that spills over the border

Trash the skin we shed and shed,
and over it grows, and over it grows—

Trash the forest. Trash the reef that whitens the sea,
that drags the sky, that flaps
its baggy wings in the branches of trees

Trash this language
that clutters, that eddies and snags, and whelps
its litter in hoarded places

Trash this mouth that undecomposes

This mouth now waiting to howl

to know a thing

Irène Mathieu

every poem I write is about the same thing:
how ordinary it is to want a long line of sunrises,
bowls of oatmeal with you—in other words

what my parents have collected—
while the world goes on dying.
who am I to wish for more life
than even this slow-burning planet?

some days I feel so useless
even though I have called my senators multiple times.
it's horrible the ways we can be to each other,
and what of my surprise when someone I think
wants me dead or very far away
speaks kindly to me. what does my surprise say?
at this point in history I have a shield for a face.

if consciousness is a large animal we feed
while living in its softly breathing belly
then it is stuffed sick, the stomach bloating
into long-suffering lungs, the paws
fumbling in old dirt for a sanctified center.

it wants to feel it, clumsily, to burn its paws on the
lava face of it, to bleed a little into what goes on
making us, even though some days we don't recycle
and there are still people without homes.

the plates under us slowly shift,
the animal takes another shallow breath,
made crazier by fear,
and even this feeling—the one I have right now—
is tired of hearing itself whine into the thinning.

here is your air full of thorns. what one
more crying does. love loves you for this,
wants to make you oatmeal, but what you two do,
really, is as original as decomposition.

the steady approach of entropy, it'll break your heart.
how like us it is to know a thing by name
and at the same time swear it's not true.

From *The City Is Lush With / Obstructed Views*
Greg Nissan

The economic cartage of night-soil
  Blinking cursor where the river
   Enters our city disguised in
    No, it's original. Researchers place
    Oat flakes on a map
     To watch slime mold reconstruct
     The railways. What doesn't match
     They suggest we amend. Blinking
     Cursor where the river ends
         returns again

    *

Then a most unusual thing
  Commissioned as a tampered acanthus.
  I did not make it
   New. I didn't make it
   At all. We find a
    Bench near the falls to
    Watch the falls. Must I
    Fill in the river's blank?
    Bang bang bang. That's the
        thanks talking

*

After you're dead it pays
  For itself. Mulch, be mouth.
   Mouth, be be. Ciao, baby.
    I signal a left turn
     On the television, history is
      Turn on the television. Laddered
       Flesh I mean sitting watching
        The day go day. It
         Pays to collectivise frustration, tart
                the lemons

*

Should I rewrite them in
 A lyric mode i.e. deteriorating
  Ratio of acacia to K-hole?
   JK. I'm aching to invade
    Night one must imagine the
     Streetlights saying. It's an impossible
     Game. It's over. The hills.
      No justice. NO FILTER. To
       Get us all in, turnstiles
                demand embrace

*

Lake lake lake lake lake
 The shorn ablution. Disfrutar its
  Proof-sick city its capsuled
   Axiality, a red sign that
    Reads WATER it's a mixed
     Aquifer but what sieves in
      Leaves juridical patinas. Let's meet
       In another life, I'm busy
        Finding an apartment. Green gate,
         draped charnel

*

A horrible ending I continue
 Drizzling kill-counts along the canal
  In theory the lamplight distends
   No, it's original. Dappled in
    Juridical moonlight, a stone admits
     NO FILTER. It's that simple.
      Terraces full of alluring air
       Rights. It's my life: it's
        Never. Chafed bricks made accusative
         thanks, weather

The Golden Hour

Rowan Ricardo Phillips

Wait. So you're new? Great.
I've always wanted to show someone around.
Here: If you look straight up you'll see
The tops of skyscrapers
Staring straight down at you
And the sidewalks you thought you were walking on
Are actually way up there in the high distance.
I know, right? Look at them,
All like the concrete vapor trails of thousands
Of concrete passing planes, and here: look down,
See your hands where your feet
Should be and nothing where your hands
Should be and nothing in your pockets anyway?
Awesome. Welcome to the First Light. Enjoy
The feeling while it lasts.
Because soon this will all be normal to you
And you will feel as normal as *&#%
And believe me that will #$*!&^@ suck. Look at this:
It's just like CGI. Touch me,
Oh, that's right: you have no hands.
Imagine touching me. It's much better that way
anyway. Anyway. . .
Yeah. No. It doesn't rain anymore. But
There's the sun up there maybe perhaps.
And every golden hour (I don't know what that is),

Like clockwork (I mean, right?), they
Have their people shake their trashcans
Out their windows
And the coins that make it down here
They feel kind of a little bit like rain.
They call it watering the money tree.
I'm just happy to be in the way.

Successor

Gyrðir Elíasson

When the mammoth
realized its final
day was coming, it tried
to survive by fleeing.
But it was too laden,
and everywhere it traveled
was tundra, the faint sun half
sunken behind the horizon.
It was the very last of its kind
pursued
by the first men.

—Translated from the Icelandic by Meg Matich

Reflections on the Law of Causation

Gyrðir Elíasson

We'll never know anything
unless the killer at slaughter
is reborn as a lamb
driven through the autumn chill
into the cold bed of a truck
by biting dogs

—Translated from the Icelandic by Meg Matich

Life After Nature

Gyrðir Elíasson

When the pass to the valley opens,
it quickly becomes apparent that the grass
has been replaced with astroturf. It's swayed
by wind, warmed by a heat-lamp
sun. Man-made rivers
run through the valley.
Blades of grass whisper the incessant
static of a radio
station. In the evening, the lamps
are switched off, but the whispers
persist.
You can't change
the channel.

—Translated from the Icelandic by Meg Matich

Chicken Smog

Nicole Walker

There are days when I clutch at the Great Sadness as if it will give
me something to eat. A chicken drumstick to gnaw on as I go

through my day sorting out this excellent blue
sky from this less excellent brown one. I don't mind,

really, the way the tendon gets stuck in my teeth. I have
spoken about love and cruelty before. I know this floss

well. A line that demarcates teeth is the same line
that divides sun from smog. It wouldn't be a world,

at least not our world, if we didn't have chicken parts
to organize it. My mother is selling her condo in Salt Lake.

I'm looking into buying a bigger house so she can move in
with me. Where do the Salt Laken mothers

live when they come? The kids' rooms, I guess,
which is fine except the cats sleep in there and Erik

sleeps with the dogs and I sleep upstairs dreaming
of chickens. Good chickens with their legs still

attached, eating vegetarian like they should, like we
all should if we are good people but we're not

that good so we take the legs and wings off
of the bird. I like the kind with hot sauce

from Buffalo or the thighs with skin broiled.
I eat them alone in my bedroom. All skin.

I like breasts grilled and all the body smoked.
The whole body roasted. Once, I tried to make

a fricassee. I left the stove for just one minute
to go to the bathroom (I promise I washed my hands),

but when I came out I'd burnt the garlic. The skin
of the chicken thighs too was charred and venting

upward even though I have a downdraft vent and I
thought maybe this is how they can fix Salt Lake's

smog problem. Downdraft. Worst air quality in the nation. Known
by the Paiute tribe as the smoky valley, that place in winter

always socked in thick but now with the oil refineries
and two million cars pumping particulates into

that smoke the whole valley is a murky soup
thicker and more punishing than the Great Salt

Lake which is its own kind of sinking problem.
All the mercury in the world wants to land

there. Heavy bottom. Lower than salt. Imagine how we could,
in a drought, the summer-end of the smog problem, suck

that broiled sky into the Great Salt Lake
glimmering with the promise (lie) of water, the suggestion

that maybe this one place will survive the great drying (sink
carbon. Sink mercury) of the west. That lake

you can see from outer space and then you hike
out to the shore only to find it is as good and useful

as the over-seasoned chicken you burned last night.
I took the problem, with a bucket of fried chicken,

not from KFC but from Meiers the last night,
to my mom's condo she loved because

we could sink deeply into outdoor furniture. We did sit
right on the patio, paper napkins flying everywhere,

bees diving for the chicken and she said, "Maybe this
isn't the only place to live. Maybe it's not even the best

place." Which is exactly what the chicken thought
at the Tyson food factory and is exactly the thought we choked

down even though we didn't mean it at all. It was only
three in the afternoon. Not warm enough for patio-sitting.

Not warm enough for bees. We went inside for the last
time because the dark was coming early. You could barely

divine the sun out in this entirely non-excellent smog time.
Nothing to see and nowhere to sleep and the difference between

everything, including the chicken and especially the day, blurred.
I can't forever rely on my mom to tell me when it's morning.

Preview

Rae Armantrout

1

There are worldwide, catastrophic storms
when earth's network
of weather-control satellites
is sabotaged by unknown enemies.

As fire rages through the western forest
Jeff Bridges snarls,
"If you want a piece of me,
come get me."

2

The baby says, "MMM, MMM!"
to the stuffed fish
then hits it
against her closed mouth.

"Ah, Ah," she says,
holding it at a distance.

She opens and closes
the palm of one hand. "Bye-bye,"
we say for her.
"Bye-bye, Fishy!"

Signs You Are Standing at the End

Abigail Chabitnoy

Two-thirds of the country is in drought. The waters have all gone walking.

Nunakuarluni. Take a hike.

When white peaks crested the rolling hills behind our house

I knew it was time.

We understand since we are children waves break waves travel waves do the wave. Did the wave make it across the room? Did the people who started it move across the room?

Cause of death: traumatized. Cause of death: bad heart. Cause of death: exposure.[1]

(I heard it was an accident. In the end. In the breakers. There was no boat when they told it.)

I took my brother and sister and some others out the back door. The calm was not and the neatly kept lawn was not.

The sleeper wave was not.

---

1 To the cold air; to want of sea ice; to warming air; to a landscape without trees; too many ribs; to the sea; to ghosts; to loss of stable earth to plant one's feet, one's seed, one's egg, one's teeth.

Too many teeth I saw too late. The wave would not be dove under.

It turned snow, wet and heaving and we
                                              were already running.

*

After, a field. I could hear every dead thing.

                    How do we behave in the field?

They asked for a story, the ones we'd have to leave behind. Swallowed
by the hoary mouth.
Never ignore what someone tells you in a dream, once the women said.
You are trying to remember what someone said
                                              who is dead.

Quliyangua'uciikamken. — I will tell you a story.

                    Laam'paaq kuarsgu.

it looks like driftwood but, really, it's an apocalypse

Matt Massaia

A single grain a second. This ice cream kind of night, the horizon
the softest flavor I can imagine and explaining to Dylan that beach
glass actually isn't sharp, it's actually incredibly smooth because
this whole place is actually sandpaper without the paper.

The beach glass a jellyfish fragmented, or a cut-away lamp
abandoned on the shore, or maybe given to the drowned to hang
around and listen. Bird track trails for hours, we were following
them and I was looking for a piece of beach glass to show Dylan,

and when I found it and he turned it over in his hand he was surprised
that it was so smooth. This nature filing down the sharp edges
is the easy human thing to say. The beach, the proxy agent of that
old binary nature. A beach that can't catch a virus the way

computers can, but still file down Grandpa's Heineken, and this brown
yellow piece of glass, this honey that I've captured here, that splits
my hand open. Yellowstone could erupt—it's long overdue for busting
loose, but the nuclear winter would create a cloud shield, subverting

our careless carbon suicide-bomb. We'd freeze for seven years, sure.
Most of western North America and its populations would probably
die or else contract pneumonoultramicroscopicsilicovolcanoconiosis,
but goodbye global warming, hello wool sweaters if I can find a living

sheep to collect from. This animal that owes me a debt, this thought that won't be returned to me. I'm terrified of anthropomorphizing the sheep or the volcano because I wish to not do them violence, but fuckers I can't trust that you wouldn't treat me by remarking the curls

of my hair are horns, and calling my feet hooves, but who can I be to say what language you're using. It doesn't matter how a word like "nature" is defined if that definition has already swallowed everything, like my mouth on my finger, sucking a sharp spot dry.

After Nature

Roger Reeves

The miry skull of a half-eaten ram,
Viscous rapture, the wounds opening to the earth;

Below, a mole that once shouldered its blind—
Ambition, babies, fame—but now ferries his late luggage
On a spine churned to milk and pulp by pesticides;

Gethsemane sacked, bagged, and measured out
In Instagrams for shekels of bitten-through coin;

Ants auditing abundance in the outhouse of death;
Persephone promoted to pantomiming her loss
In one hundred forty characters or less

(Will you be my friend on Facebook?); owl,
Black sheep weeping for wampum, woo-woo,

And white folks' money in a flooded pasture;
Goats, all the angels, dead so Satan the only
Seer of heaven, and he, not talking; sovereign,

So sovereign the saws in the forest
They call themselves 'Pope' and 'Pious'

In the felling and working of trees from flesh to soul;
Property, property, all is property;
What was ever the wisdom in hierarchies?

How were we to practice cruelty if not with virtue?
Sing, Muse, of the disappearing world.

The Elements

Carolyn Guinzio

The elements are arguing over what we should become

The Larsen C Ice Shelf on Its Last Legs

Noah Dversdall

All last night I was up thinking what sound
a trillion pounds of ice would make when it fell in the water,
    (ice crack | no ice smack | no ice clack
    no ice clap | no ice slap | no ice snap | no ice noise
           I wouldn't hear it
        but no, cold whispers | chill wave
                   lap along the coast
                   no
                   quiet breeze and a sail
                   soft-taut in it no
                   light | no light | no light
                   landing | no light shudder | no shudder
                   no ice quake | no ice shake | no
                        I shiver thinking)
        but no, I don't understand
        but no, understand me,
        understand me, it's too dark to see
        but I want to hear the ocean rise.

I Am Chopping Ivory or Bone

Joan Naviyuk Kane

How many Eskimo words are there for *white people*? How many Eskimo words are there? How many Eskimo?

*

My mother told me to attach a string to a claw, then the other end of the string to a scrap of wood: "take the claw and put a string with a little piece of wood." I must have asked her something or paused for her to continue. Or she paused, and then continued.

"You swing it and try to put the wood through the claw." I asked her what kind of crab claw. "Crab from King Island."

*

There is a game my mother perhaps invented but certainly became adept at, as a girl, in King Island Village. With a string, dried stem, or sinew, you attached a crab claw to a smithereen of wood (even driftwood being not easy to come by) and tried to catch the claw on the small wooden stick. I asked her what kind of crabs. I think she said something about king crabs or kinds of crab, but she definitely said the words "King Island." I asked my husband later that day where he thought she got the wood. The thing upon which the crab claw balanced; not pierced or punctured.

*

How many miles from the nearest tree is King Island? How many Eskimo words for *tree* are there? How many Eskimo words? How many Eskimo? How many?

*

The evening following this conversation with my mother also followed an evening when my husband, children, and I joined my parents for dinner at

Mexico in Alaska—an Anchorage restaurant we'd chosen to frequent for forty-one years. I asked her where she was when she played this game. "King Island." Then I asked her where she got the wood. "It was around," she explained.

*

She remembered another game involving crab claws. *If it landed one way, it was a seal. If it landed another, it was a polar bear.* What do you mean? I asked. I meant, which way does it have to land for it to be a seal? For a polar bear? And what does that mean? She repeated, word for word: *If it landed one way, it was a seal. If it landed another, it was a polar bear.* Does this mean a hunter would get a seal or a polar bear? As in, stalk and harvest and bring back to store up or share with others? Or that the crab claw held the innate *inua* of a *niqsaq* or a *nanuaq*? Asking these question in English substituting three Inupiaq words for three English words didn't prompt any further explanation or conversation. Is the use of Eskimo words an event?

*

There are two modes of narrative in the tradition of Inupiaq literature: *quliapyuk* and *unipkaaq*. Yaayuk Alvanna-Stimpfle translates *quiliapyuk* as story and *unipkaaq* as legend. Larry Kaplan, director of the Alaska Native Language Center and a linguist fluent in the King Island dialect of the Inupiaq language, explains that the former "includes oral history and personal reminiscence, usually relating something the storyteller or someone he knows has experienced," and that the latter "is an ancient myth," one that "tells of events, often with supernatural aspects, which occurred long before anyone can remember." My mother and most of my other relatives have the habit of speaking about experiences on King Island in the third-person past tense, which, aside from being accurate (most King Islanders left the island in 1959, no one has lived on the island year-round since 1965, and the number of surviving King Islanders born after 1974 who have been to the island could probably be counted on two hands) always troubled me with its emphasis on fixing hundreds or thousands of years of habitation of the island in the distant and impersonal and irrecoverable past.

Part of this has to do with the suffix *-guuq*, which translates most passively into English as "it is told" or "it is said." In the context of a conversation, or storytelling session, to hear this verbal terminative would be a way to reaffirm the preceding utterance's legitimacy by having the authority of its assertion rest outside of the subjective and limited perspective (and perhaps motivations) of the speaker. It would be a way for the speaker to remind the listener that these words were spoken. They happened. They are real, and connect the listener to some kind of truth. They're not an invitation to historicize, to impel the speaker to use an active voice, to needlessly distort or omit.

*

There are two books I need to mention as long as I seem to have your attention: Joseph Senungetuk's *Give or Take a Century* and William Oquilluk's *People of Kauwerak*. The former can be read as a memoir of the author's formative years in Nome, Alaska, and his family's history and engagement with the land around Wales, Alaska. It was published in 1971 and I could not imagine being a writer without this book. The latter was published in 1973 and I would not be alive without this book, without the events it chronicles. It recounts with vivid and verifiable detail the five historical disasters the Inupiaq people have survived and continue to survive.

I was, along with my children and husband, once at Oquilluk's house in Homer. While there I proudly spoke the Inupiaq language with my sons, Joe and Ron, who had learned it as young men in Nome. "The kind of Inupiaq your grandfather spoke," Oquilluk told me, "was like Shakespeare's English."

Oquilluk, along with my maternal grandmother and her two sisters (and hundreds of other Inupiaq children), was orphaned in the 1918 influenza pandemic and raised by Ursuline nuns at a Catholic orphanage on the grounds of Pilgrim Hot Springs on Alaska's Seward Peninsula. The virus traveled from village to village with postal delivery from Nome. Death letters. All the orphans raised in the orphanage became fluent in English: a full bilingualism. And then, French. German. Latin. Other (e)vocables. Locutions. Things overheard. And things to read.

*

Back in the last century, I was one of the first employees of the Alaska Native Heritage Center, where we were given a script that was written (by a white anthropologist) for us to deliver in the third-person past tense to an audience that consisted largely of cruise-ship tourists. Paradoxically, the Heritage Center, owned by a regional Alaska Native corporation, has developed most of its local land—the boreal forest in Anchorage—into big box stores and strip malls. Anyhow, the script was comprehensive and detailed, and not to be whimsically spruced up with the interruption of personal narrative.

I was a college student, slightly bored and wondering what my friends in NYC and Boston were up to. What my relatives were doing on the tundra or the swelling tides of the Bering Sea, in the endless light of summer's white nights. I needed to depart from the script for the sake of my sanity, even though we were monitored and reprimanded for such departures. One of the things I was required to do was to demonstrate "Eskimo yo-yo" in order to increase the sales of authentically handcrafted yo-yo products in the Heritage Center's gift shop. Once I got the tourists interested in how fun and rewarding it was to master their use, I would tell the tourists the real story of how my mom and uncles and most other King Islander kids would play with grass-filled, skin-stitched, and fur-tufted yo-yos (not dissimilar from the poly-filled ones available for sale in the gift shop just to the right of the exit) in order to later better use bone- or rock-weighted bolas to catch and kill migratory seabirds for food, clothing, fun, ceremony, stewardship, exchange, ornament, pedagogy, or all of these and more. There were millions of birds that nested on King Island. I didn't understand *millions* in any language until I went to King Island myself. That is another story, all those birds and all the things and places and people that could still be there, or maybe definitely once were, but already and definitely may not be and may, in the grand scheme of things, never even have existed. This could all be vacant any instant.

*

I imagine the cliffs bare.

"Mom," I ask, after a good interval of conversation where we both repeat things to each other we already know, "is there a word you know for seabird?" Maybe she doesn't want to disappoint me. "*Imaani*: ocean. *Tiŋmiat*: bird. *Imaani.tiŋmiat*," she answers.

*   *   *   * *   * *   ** *

How many oceans full of seabirds were there?
How many oceans
How many words

     many oceans once full of seabirds
     few words to describe them

     tiŋitkaa: it blew away
     a particular constellation containing many stars: *siġupsiġat*
     siġvauraq: young guillemot
     it is empty: *imailaq*
     imiktuq: it is echoing

qayuktuŋa

an empirical formula of intangibles

Ellen Welcker

that the lungs continue to inflate
that that which sustains us kills us
that this morning a gun in a school bathroom
that the bluster of little men
that winter's harshness, unimaginable and near
that summer's tragedies, elsewhere and here
that an errant arrow in my neighborhood
that a basketball is a pig bladder
that a pig bladder is a human lung
in the alley behind the garage
that the world of the invisible is real
includes feelings, threats, and air
that that which sustains us, kills us
that at any given point there is no actual
that being is crystalline and mutable
is gas is solid is liquid
is full and devoid of feeling
as you wish
that all of this is true
of animals, rocks, and plants
that the bluster of little men
and earth is the loneliest place
that to be is empirically lonely
that is, a planet, or on one
that loneliness is not the same as aloneness

that empire is aloneness
that empire alone will kill us, is killing us
and it is difficult and necessary to die
a little or a lot
that to ask of oneself a death
is not a small thing or lonely
that that which kills us sustains us
that the lungs continue to inflate

From *Shale Plays*
Ted Mathys

Lessons learned can be shared and modified from play to play, [but] each
one has distinct properties which require custom approaches in order to
maximize gas and oil recovery.
—Halliburton

. . . oh, yes, yes, the matter goes on, // turning into this and that, never
the same thing twice: / but what about the spirit . . .
—A. R. Ammons

Fracking Fayetteville

Acid scours the wellbore. Water-soluble guar
to regulate viscosity. South to north on U.S. 65,
a fleet of 300 carbon steel tankers is alive
with 400 million gallons of alluvial aquifer.

Poseidon's dominion is both ocean and earthquake
but the Ozarks aren't Greek. In a contrary direction
the farmer's trident pitchfork leans in his barn
while he swallows the lease. The play goes bulimic.

Radioactive flowback is pooled in ponds—
benzene, xylene, naphthalene—spread on fields,
re-injected beneath his rooster's bloodline song.

Two counties away, an Iraq vet with PTSD
braces for the next tremor in a beige La-Z-Boy.
He watches a documentary about the tides and sea.

Fracking Niobrara

When a pointillist blob of fossil fuel wells
overwhelms my laptop map of the play,
I exit the café and find an actual fossil, gray
trilobite sealed in a decorative pebble.

I take it home for my daughter's terrarium.
It now lives with what else has died but lives
again in glass—a hawk feather, crisp leaves,
a pine cone, a robin's nest, and freshwater clam

on a bed of ghost-white aquarium gravel.
Some nights, when I come home to a house
asleep, my emptiness fixed on its own completion,

I lift the small lid and run my finger down
the trilobite's washboard segments. I can only
bring myself to do this when all the lights are out.

Fracking Granite Wash

The swath of lithologies is shaped like a mitten
knitted around the hand of the past. The palm
blooms in supplication, as if to take alms
or admit an invisible methane pigeon

to crosswind. The pigeon banks, flails,
a fugitive emission from the tight-gas basin
in flight from custody, justice, vigilante citizens,
arrest. Convicted in absentia, the bird jumps bail,

detectable only by a thermal camera's spectral
infrared. The force that shot the blossom
through the green fuse drives her pinions

into atmospheric gas. She diffuses. Her wingspan's
global, centimeter-thin, and denied on C-SPAN
as a weather anomaly of hurricane proportion.

Fracking Haynesville

FAUST
    Come in then!

MEPHISTO
    That's the spirit.

        —Goethe

88 MPH on a road he knows, no seat belt, no
phantom medical episode, the shale-gas CEO
plows into an overpass. Rigged to run on CNG,
his Tahoe explodes. A permanent shadow

sears into ragweed. Afterglow in Riyadh,
in Caracas. The black box captures vehicle
data, but motivation creates epistemological
crisis. It cannot know that he was indicted

the day before for conspiring to rig leases,
or that NatGas stocks rally on news of his death,
or that eight years prior the Sierra Club chairman,

to depose King Coal, accepted his $26 million
in donations. *Conspire*: to breathe together,
spirit of the demos that whispers "come in."

Fracking Marcellus

One of the things I kinda like is my stuff leads to a volatile conclusion.
—Quentin Tarantino on *Pulp Fiction*

Cinephiles debate the boreal glow
emitted by Marsellus Wallace's stolen
briefcase. A baby nuke, gold bullion,
an Oscar, Elvis's golden lamé tuxedo,

a 60-watt soft white or Marsellus's soul
extracted from a borehole in his neck,
overlaid with a Band-Aid. Vincent
Vega pops the combination: 666,

luminesces from the contents, later
gets wasted by Butch. But in the diner,
with a .45 in his face, Jules

```
        flips the locks and opens the case, revealing
        it to Pumpkin but not to us. The same light
        SHINES from the case. Pumpkin's expression
        goes to amazement. Honey Bunny, across the
        room, can't see shit.

                    HONEY BUNNY
            What is it? What is it?
```

                    PUMPKIN
                   (softly)
          Is that what I think it is?

     Jules nods his head: "yes."

                    PUMPKIN
              It's beautiful.

     Jules nods his head: "yes."

                    HONEY BUNNY
          Goddammit, what is it?

The Trial

Carolyn Guinzio

Do you ever fear that everything you fear is true

is true

Among Some Anapests at Civic Center

Brenda Hillman

(including a line by Tobias Meneley)

The fascists have entered the town

      Sun like a late   ripe peach

      City says no
      to masks

We go with the crows & the crowd
      A defensive line is made

My telomeres   all lined up

The State prepares the tear gas canisters
      (almost wrote teenage canisters)

My pronoun is wearing a mask
A defensive line is made

We go with the G & the H

Poets are often tired
We don't think the hitting will work
We grow calm   among the zeroes

My house was a little too calm
       Our telomeres all lined up

i'm too old to jump over walls

A terrible beauty is dead

& the sun was tender upon us

i don't think the hitting will work
A defensive time is made

A poem is not a protest

The Nazis have entered the park

Subject to history's impress

My telomeres all lined up—
       Subject to cosmic rays

Aw Aw awe awe crows say

My house was a little too calm
Was thinking of Nicolás Guillén

Was thinking of William Blake

We go with the crows & the crowd
Hate hate hate hate free speech

i'm too old to jump over walls

A defensive line is made
   Subject to history's impress

i don't think the hitting will work

Changed utterly wrote Yeats

Sun like a late   ripe peace

The State unfolds the tear gas thermoses
We follow the crows   **Awe Aw**

A defensive line is made
A defensive line is made
My house was a little too calm
A defensive line is made
i follow the crows & the qualm

repeat repeat repeat

Aubade

Kaveh Akbar

Pardon my asking, but do you think I could drink
this and be okay? I am still learning the scents

of poisons, can't yet smell them in the wild. Sip it
and tell me if you die. I've heard

you can make tea from almost anything:
the mist on a cobweb, a tongue cut

from a corpse. We bodies carry so much
flavor inside ourselves—the unborn

gorge and pulse in their glee. Can I say I like
you best when you share yourself, when you

lend me a comb or toss me your jaw? I trust
you completely, with your bruised lungs

rattling like stones in a jug. Some birds
have feathers in their hearts, I'm not

making that up. When we met you were wearing
a purple cashmere mask studded with fake

diamonds. You said *hold still, tyrant!* and tackled
me to the ground. It was awful. Love,

don't we seem yellower today? Don't we seem
fungal and more complex? Every generation,

man's eyes get smaller, less able to detect
danger in the periphery. It's a handsome

predicament: we are born with the ways
we will die already built in. Don't bother

with the copperhead in the garden
or the giant black eyeball rolling through

the tall grass. The only thing to do now is cheer
louder, fill our pockets with shells. You

were supposed to warn me before
you discovered the ark—it would have been nice

to dig up together. I have spent years
perfecting my helpless face, my every-beast-

of-the-earth face. I guess it's just that lately
I have been feeling so poorly seen. I let

the sun set on my confusion and wake covered
in a film of feather grease. Tiny hunter,

little hole-in-a-leaf, you have always been
doomed, the meat of my gaze. I am

a tractor trailer with the heart of a living
boy. I am doing all of this to myself.

12:41 p.m.

Ellen Welcker

Our friend tells us about the childhood game
called "bag of danger."
Outside the sky is August,
the weather is smoke, the color is yellow,
the boy at the bus stop's dad is buying coffee.
He is hard on his weird little child.
Someone says, *she contains multitudes,*
everyone chuckles. My son
would like to have a gun birthday.
He modifies, as he is wont to,
because of my face, its bags of wonder
and fatigue morphing incredulously:
There will only be one gun, he says,
it's a love gun, it shoots noodles, well—
it shoots bullets, but the bullets will just be
little plastic things. Harmless then.
Or not. Last night a splinter shot
from my heel, an inch long, had been
lurking, unseen, like the thing I have
in my blood. As do multitudes. The men
posture and snort and all the coastal peoples
lie awake. The mother is texting, *do you want this,*
do you want this. The child puts the phone
in her pocket. The men speak of lessons
and fury. Behind them is a time, less memorable

than the Mesozoic, or Paleozoic, a time
of pre-mammals, and an ocean of thick
strong shells. A time when the thing a child
now fears—some remainder of the brain's
evolutionary bag of tricks—turned the sea
into a sack of death; the sky, something
unbreathable. Today we are in the orange zone:
fine particulate matter is the matter,
which makes my lungs two bags
of danger. She put everything she could think of
in there, placed it at the center of the playground,
flicked a Bic, and ran. The weird little child
is crying. He doesn't want to have to always go
on a mission to find her. A mission, thinks the mother,
incredulously. Her eyes are filmed
with particulate, her heels and toes catch on the sheets.
At 9:15 the men dropped Little Boy on Hiroshima.
Three days later, at 11:02, Fat Man on Nagasaki.
In the living room, right now, at 12:41, the child
is sobbing: *I'm so mad, I'm so mad, something*
is the matter inside me and I don't know what.

A Dedication

Christopher Nelson

To you of the unimaginable
tomorrow, we loved as you will love

as you will find it a way to
endure the banishment

into the singular island of a body
that will be gently

worn to failure, like a solid pier
by the touch of waves

which regard their work as
constant encouragement. To you

for whom these words will be
quaint and lacking

the magnitude of your vibrant
now, it is night for me.

I open the window despite
January to hear the voices

of the few passersby
stolen by wind and smothered

by the rush of cars.
Gas is $2.79 a gallon and I

am 42 years. Carlos is lost. Shayma
and Sharif unable to return.

Jacob, Michael, Gabe, Juanita,
Blas. I still see Sky,

before the bullet un-
wound time, the pink hat she wore

that Tuesday in the rain.

Security Camera Disguised as Birdhouse

Diana Keren Lee

your life is divided into fifteen-second clips
the sound of all your pauses
o lonely one shed the worm
the toxic green of blockbuster films
time needs something to kill too
positive capability is the tree
bowing in broken Korean
where an old riot was never recorded
bird of paradise a bright orange slice through your eye
the camouflage now pixelated like your quick response
the robot thinks he knows he's not a pawn
dyslexia in dystopia
the socioeconomic as seriocomic
security camera disguised as birdhouse

Godo

Adam Day

catalyzed by Claude Lanzmann's *Shoah* (1985)

This was not
the world. I was told

that these
are human

beings—they did not
look like

human beings.

From *Mere Life: An Algorithmic Poem* *with* *Human Additions*

Kyle Booten

Shamus child of Ewan and Lyn found a dead beast and ate it. Shoshie child of Ansel and Jimbo stole a beak from Gillan child of Kevan and Ewan. Ewan child of Sanderson and Ashlen gave a scarab shell to Addie child of Jodi and Selma. Gillan child of Kevan and Ewan found zinc. Si child of Barbara and Jordan gave a beak to Wat child of Thatch and Kevan. Carrol child of Teriann and Lyn gave sand to Kissie child of Sigfried and Jamey: say my name, say my name. Helen child of Hendrik and Archibold found a dead beast and ate it. Jimbo child of Tommi and Thaddus gave a scarab shell to Ansel child of Helen and Rosario. Quintus child of Si and Jimbo found mud. Isadore child of Zebulon and Rosario found a beak. Magdaia child of Fleurette and Selma found sand. Mufinella child of Bridie and Carrol found a beak. Jori child of Ashlen and Tim gave a nest to Briggs child of Eveline and Alanah. Jori child of Ashlen and Tim and Briggs child of Eveline and Alanah begat Quincy and hoped that one day he might meet the shore. Addie child of Jodi and Selma found mud. Zebulon child of Tommi and Thaddus found a dead beast and ate it. Putting aside the image of Zebulon's fingers sinking into the beast, the economic nature of this transaction is worth pausing to appreciate: 1) The act of eating a dead beast is revolting. 2) The production of dead beasts, fallen animals that are explicitly not meat, cannot be easily taken over by traditional forms of meatification such as hunting or large-scale beast farming. In that sense dead beasts are more like truffles or sapphires than hamburgers. 3) Therefore each discovery of a dead beast is experienced outside of traditional markets. Each dead beast is, to the beholder, a stinking miracle. 4) Eventually these beasts become luxury items and the consumers develop a vocabulary to describe the way that this delicacy is not just unrevolting but in fact several times more delicious than corn, simple breads, and chicken. Not accidentally, the class that benefits most from consuming dead beasts is also the most vociferous in its defense of belles-lettres. Thaddus child of Laverne and Harmonia found mud. Teriann child of Carin and Jimbo found mud. Kissie child of Sigfried and Jamey found sand. Laurianne child of Ansel and Carrol found a lullaby. Sleep became very important. Lancelot child of Tammie and Eliot found mud. Thomas child of Helen and Selma gave iron ore to Evey child of Jamey and Alanah. Marilyn child of Thatch and Vachel gave a nest to Aurore child of Zebulon and Charlot. Vivyan child of Katina and Fleurette found a dead beast and ate it. Armed with a rock, Toddy child of Tommi and Tallia came upon Addie child of Jodi and Selma, and so, at age four Addie child of Jodi and Selma was no more: this was not the first time Toddy had seen Addie, who so often wandered down by the stream to practice fishing with melodies such as ˘ ˘ ˘ ˘ as well as others improvised to pluck the piscine death drive, though there was always a danger of drawing too much on one's own feelings and experiences. Sigfried child of Jordan and Rosario gave a nest to Alanah child of Tim and Kevan. Sigfried child of Jordan and Rosario and Alanah child of Tim and Kevan begat Powell. Briggs child of Eveline and Alanah found a nest. Eveline child of Humphrey and Jimbo found iron ore. Amelita child of Shamus and Helen found a rock. Fleurette child of Laverne and Lucius gave a mercury droplet to Barris child of Ashlen and Thomas. Fleurette child of Laverne and Lucius and Barris child of Ashlen and Thomas begat Charyl. Thatch child of Jimbo and Teriann gave sand to Amelita child of Shamus and Helen. Thatch child of Jimbo and Teriann and Amelita child of Shamus and

Helen begat Wallace, also referred to as the glutton, carcajou, skunk bear, or quickhatch. Scotty child of Jori and Jamey found a dead beast and ate it. Emmalynne child of Helen and Jordan found a rock. Wat child of Thatch and Kevan found a dead beast and ate it. Sholom child of Aubrey and Blanch found fire. Humphrey child of Emmalynne and Eliot found a dead beast and ate it. Carleigh child of Marilyn and Ebony and Ebony child of Carrol and Toddy begat Glenn. Ingeberg child of Quintus and Verge stole mud from Jordan child of Betteanne and Sanderson and wept when it did not burn, and she tried to eat it but it wouldn't go down. Jodi child of Tallia and Tim and Nanci child of Laverne and Denna begat Evie. Tallia child of Jimbo and Wain gave a quick beast to Jori child of Ashlen and Tim. Tallia child of Jimbo and Wain and Jori child of Ashlen and Tim begat Christoph. Charyl child of Fleurette and Barris and Carrol child of Teriann and Lyn begat Terina and Carrol knew that he would protect Terina at all costs, armed with all sharp rocks, with all stealth and thievery, with all eagles crashing down upon enemies and strangers, all strangers his enemies, all enemies void and unnamed. Wallace child of Thatch and Amelita and Teriann child of Carin and Jimbo begat Vik. Evie child of Jodi and Nanci found a beak. Terina child of Charyl and Carrol found a seed and ate it.

maron

Irène Mathieu

girl in a swamp
getting too free for her body,
lets her knotted stomach turn to wood,
her skin to bark.

the barking gets closer, so she lowers her rifle into
the water, lethal nose first, and it slips under.

her shrinking feet sniff for home and find it.
girl, who shot at an angry man, is becoming
not-girl in answer to the neck's question.

she calls down thunder and her fingernails become buds.
rain confuses the dogs, who whimper and turn in circles.

her toes stretch into the soil, become hollow, drink.
her digits unfurl, translucent tongues communing with air.
girl is on the way to becoming a common fig.

she closes her eyes.
the men are shouting obscenities,
prodding the dogs with rifle butts.

the common fig does not normally grow in a swamp,
but humans will also give birth in caves, wrap the umbilical cord

with vine to separate child from open-mouthed bayou,
will hold their breath underwater for eighteen minutes
while armed men scour the shore,
and will be the mosquitoes' sacrificial flesh,
offer themselves to needling proboscises—
before they would return to not-free.

the swamp is speaking, so she nods her branches in reply,
introduces herself, a blooming idiosyncrasy.

from her not-hands drop ripe figs.
they split open in the rain.

the dogs have arrived.
they lick her bark, confused, chew the fruity pulp.

the men catch up, scratch their heads.

the girl has escaped.

Object Project

Tracy Fuad

Finally I am feeling the soft cramps of menstruation

Another red start

Another spreadsheet where every cell is a day containing local weather

It all adds up to a project

What about a war that only lasts five hours?

Still the pixels green and die

Still I navigate to objectsobjectsobjects.com

In eighth grade geometry I learned to hate the sound of *trace* emerging
   from beneath my teacher's mustache

A wobbly copy of a circle

I am still interested in simulation

In trying to understand a thing by recreating it in small scale

This epidemic isn't real, I tell my students as I use an eyedropper to
   indicate who is diseased

They hold their plastic cups out toward me and the ones containing
   water laced with soda ash turn vivid fuchsia and they scream

Terror is infectious, too

My final project, I decide, will be planting

I dreamt of wildflowers again

The bird said, if I seize you I will seize you and will squeeze you till
   you squirt

Well, not actually, but that's a trick to easily identify this bird by name

The warbling vireo, a tiny songbird

I identified the bird using a video that captured the sound of the camera
   zooming in to find the bird, metal against metal, singing *kkkkkkr*

The river thrilled me, I would tell you
This thing runs all day, I said
Sometimes it feels it isn't me who's speaking when I speak
Well, I am my own personal stranger
My own personal jerk emails me to say that *videographer* seems reductive
and "idk what happened but it happened"
and that he "like(d) having me as a friend"
and signed off *fart noise*
which is the part that made me sad, that asterisk jacket
I read that song diversity predicts the viability of fragmented bird
      populations
Whether they will live in the face of widespread anthropogenic habitat
      destruction
Basically the birds aren't learning songs the way they used to
And they're dying
A bird's birdsong is its species' language, special
I want this in this poem though it is already a poem
The birds, I mean, the singing
I learned to hide my body when I was a girl
How to be a highway and rest stop and dirt road and all-at-once
I believe that recreation is dangerous
As evidence: The Oregon Trail, developed as an educational computer
      game
As evidence: I grew up on Cherokee Trail
As evidence: in fourth grade I made *mastaw* for heritage day and
      everyone spit it out in front of me
It was sour, white
I've been writing this for years
If I had known

If I didn't have to write this then I wouldn't and I'd find some other
    project
Whose idea was it to hold a heritage day?
Well, I've taught and failed children too
I hadn't known until that day how *sour* yogurt is
Sometimes italics really sting
In Kurdish *mastaw* means yogurt-water
Mast is yogurt, *aw* is water, and together they mean exactly what they
    mean
My mother called to say she is officially a master naturalist
She earned her certificate by tagging and weighing native birds
That was her final project
She said that a bird's body feels mostly empty in the hand
I have seams in places where I put myself together
No one ever thinks about harming the body as a practice of observing
    healing
How many times did my body have to heal before I believed in believing?
I dreamt of wildflowers again
The kind that grow where they are strewn out of the bag
I have the bag
I have the seeds and bulbs and hands

Mouthing Green

Emelia Reuterfors

1)

lacewings
flaunt their bodies
on the car hood. how daring
     to open
       when translucent.
silky glands
make stainless eggs.

      night rotations, darling

they shift gears. they sift
     the weak and surface.

2)

the red center
pulsed   permissions
a milky shiver for me.

i thought i saw a tongue float
like a cobweb. i thought
a worm had deepened in my throat.

        i heard something grind inside.

i take this seriously
as green-lighted prey.

locked horns, a tickling kind of
fur   is open to attack.

3)

what is discovery? teeth
inside and living
soft signatures.

we unraveled our wet
beddings   on the truck bed

glowing through the windshield, breasts divided
        just some eyes
        with singing legs.

4)

i hear what i see and it twins;
it halves in drainage,
suckles the earth's
neck, swallows
          my breath. here
is the microbic
green throat
of a throat
swallowing
a throat.

From *Aase's Death*

Aase Berg

To Nothing

Pale intestine releases a bubble.
There's a fish eye in the bubble.
That fish has no eye.
Nothing hurts.
Remember nothing,
nothing exists.

Cold Clock, Flawed Brain

They are probably never unhappy
However they will grow old
The negative water cannot freeze
at oxygen-poor depths
Time follows another pace
Birth happens sporadically
The islands north of Siberia
consist only
of mammoth bones

Sludge Dust

Slack-grubbing in the dust,
breathing out stirs up the well sludge
from the bottom muck
Nothing glows, nothing is visible.
Still I see everything. But feel nothing.
You can stick your hand
straight through me.

—Translated from the Swedish by Johannes Göransson

Diary of the Ghost of a Mestiza

Desirée Alvarez

Written in the sorcerer's house *mis palabras*

are a mutilated palace
          spread across a lake.

Elliptical pyramid. Oval. Oral.

My words are *manzanilla* crying
tea, storming the road yellow.

Mis palabras are heavy coated *coati* trundling home to the jungle.

My words are great ant hills scarring the limbs of mangroves
          My words stalk black hummocks.

I sleep by the yucca so my words can taste licorice all night.

          Mis palabras are mistletoe tangling *chechem* trees,
they fill the wood collector's bicycle cart.

Mis palabras are electrified seashells torching the dirt path
to the village smelling of dinner fire.

          They are crisp leaves of poison underfoot.

My words are plants
blooming only on moonless nights. They say

let the land stay
    and the ruin stay ruined.

        Let the vines come
        and reptiles make their slow way across the dry earth.

    Let great birds of hallucination return, and jaguars

                take back the forest.

Let us, the ruthlessly
human, retreat.

The Age of Loneliness

Evelyn Reilly

> Will we stop the destruction of the Earth . . . [or] enter a new era of its
> history, cheerfully called by some the Anthropocene, a time for and all
> about our one species alone. I prefer to call it the Age of Loneliness.
> —E. O. Wilson

Book of bark
Self as lichen
corsage
some dusty
powder on a rock
perhaps
a little shrub

Growth may mean
a piece breaks off
which may or
may not
then continue
as the same
individual

Two might merge
into each other
becoming

the same organism
within a group
for which
such distinctions
have no significance

Who stands
in these woods
feeling feelings
taught by the German
Romantic tradition

remembering once
having written
Self's name on a wall
with a handful
of glowing insects?

(So much
peacefulness
to disrupt
Meister Johann
von Goethe)

Storms of internet
outrage keep
bringing down
one dead limb
after another

while dark fruit
still sways
in remaining
winds

This poem
was just overtaken
by *This Bitter Earth*
sung by Dinah
Washington

What good is love?
mmmm

in such ruined
landscapes
with their
silenced canopies
and emptied
branches

What good is love?
mmmm

that leaves
us just
our glowing
solitude?

mmmm

The Rabbits

Jericho Brown

I caught a colony
In couples on the lawn
As I pulled into my driveway
After a night of bare music,
Of drinking on my feet
Because I think I look better
Standing. I should lie. Say
They expressed my desire
To mount and be
Mounted as they scurried
Into the darkest parts of what
I pay for, but I am tired
Of claiming beauty where
There is only truth: the rabbits
Heard me coming and said
Danger in whatever tongue
Stops them from making
More. I should say
I understood myself
That way, as danger, engine
Idling, but I thought
Infestation. Now I worry
No one will ever love me—
Furry little delights fucking

In my own front yard and I,
I am reminded of all I've gotten
Rid of. And every living
Thing that still has to go.

The Translation

Carolyn Guinzio

If you would learn our language
We would tell you what we know
If you would learn our language
We would tell you what we know

Outside the Seasons

Sheikha Helawy

In the winter, my mother used to put a bucket at the entrance to our shack.
In the morning she'd wash my face and say:
Rain water is good for your complexion.
In the summer, she would sort the underthings I hung on the laundry
    line and say:
Shame! Passersby seeing your underthings!
There is no one passing by just a herd of goats and a blind shepherd.
In the spring, I would lift my voice in song and she would rebuke me:
Enough with your craziness,
and I'm rushing after madness and justice
since falling in love with poetry.
In the fall there was nothing interesting.
Between the seasons she used to say:
Someone needs to chop the wings growing on that girl.
Don't break your brother's eye before your friends.
Outside the seasons, I learned to fly.

—Translated from the Arabic by Yosefa Raz

From *Counter-Desecration: A Glossary for Writing Within the Anthropocene**
convened by *Marthe Reed & Linda Russo*

archive: a place is an archive of its own ruins. A place is the archive of trauma as fact. It happened here. The ships came by to pick up people, their cargo and the people hauling cargo. The Pacific is our trauma and our desire. The rim is everywhere there has been a war to get caught up in—always carrying the officer's status in the body—always involved in the closed-door domesticity of empire. Your daily commute through it, or your tourist visit to it, or your wrong turn leading to it, or your binding obligation to stay in it may be a document of the place's ruin. You can sense the bodies that passed through the place before. Flown above. Eaten tunnels through. Exposed the brick and fuel spills. Paid out. Locked down. The body knows more than the curatorial eye of the drone or the tight porn shot. Or the preservation's weak references, the developers' biopolitical commitments to life. Ruins and remains post-disaster is a place of present presence, neither past nor futurist. "Which by now have turned into ruins." "He was there to collect the past."

azhigwa: now is not a time for grief or silence. the earth spits forth its seeds; new life germinates in even the narrowest crevices. the waters surface and rush. *azhigwa* is to breathe time, to thread one's hands through the atmospheric filaments. there, on the branch. a dissimulation of birds. ask them to tell their story. it is not pretense or deceit to survive a cataclysmic extinction. listen to their songs. this note, how it trills beside the next. azhigwa. we are torqued and bleeding. already. we are alive.

earth: to bring (a person) to (the) earth. To cost the earth. Earth almond. Earth art. Earth artist. Earth auger. Earth bag. Earth-baking. Earth-bank. Earth-based. Earth bath. Earth battery. Earth-bedded. Earth-beetle. Earthbind. Earth-bird. Earth-blinded. Earth-bob. Earth-bottom. Earth-bred. Earth-built. Earth-burrower. Earth car. Earth chestnut. Earth-child. Earth closet. Earth coal. Earth connection. Earth-conscious. Earth-convulsing. Earth-creeping. Earth current. Earth dam. Earth-damp. Earth day. Earth-delving. Earth-destroying. Earth-devouring. Earth-dimmed. Earth dog. Earth-drake. Earth-eating. Earth-ejected. Earth-embracing. Earth-fed. Earth-flea. Earth-flea-beetle. Earth-floored. Earthflow. Earth fly. Earth-foam. Earth-fold. Earth fork. Earth-friendly. Earth girl. Earth-glacier. Earth god. Earth goddess. Earth-hauling. Earth history. Earth hog. Earth-holder. Earth-hole. Earth hut. Earth-incinerating. Earth inductor. Earth ivy. Earth lead. Earth leakage. Earth life. Earth-line. Earth loop. Earth-lord. Earth-louse. Earth-made. Earth-magic. Earth-maker. Earth-measure. Earth-measuring. Earth-moon. Earthmoss. Earth-mound. Earth-mouse. Earth movement. Earth-noise. Earth of alum. Earth of vitriol. Earth-oil. Earth orbit. Earth-orbiting. Earth pea. Earth-piercing. Earth-pig. Earth pigment. Earth pillar. Earth plane. Earth-planet. Earth plate. Earth-pole. Earth-power. Earth-puff. Earth-refreshing. Earth resistance. Earth-rind. Earth-roofed. Earth-rooted. Earth sack. Earths-amazing. Earth satellite. Earth-scraper. Earth sculpture. Earth-sheltered. Earth sheltering. Earth shock. Earth-shrew. Earth shrinkage. Earth sign. Earthslide. Earthslip. Earth-smell. Earth-smelling. Earth smoke. Earth soul. Earth-spider. Earth spike. Earth spirit. Earth spring. Earth-sprung. Earth-squirrel. Earth-stained. Earth station. Earth-subduer. Earth-surface. Earth table. Earth-threatening. Earth throe. Earth tilting. Earth time. Earth-tint. Also calling to (the) Earth. Earth to Earth. Earth-tone. Earth tongue. Earth-treading. Earth tremor. Earth-turned. Earth-vexing. Earth-wall.

Earth-walled. Earth waller. Earth wave. Earth wax. Earth-wheeling. Earth white. Earth-wide. Earth wolf. Earth-worker. Earth-worn. Earth worship. Earth-year. The ends (also end) of (the) earth. To feel the earth move. To go to earth. To lose earth. To make the earth move.

The Great Plaints [plaint, n., roots: ME playnthe, ME plaunt, pre-seventeenth plante]: plant haunting. Conjured by uneven ecotones (echotones) carved out by homestead plows. Litany . . . *bluestem tumble-grass purpletop needleandthread buffalograss western wheatgrass switchgrass mannagrass salt grass wildrye squirreltail threadleaf sedge* . . . lamenting mass displacement of native prairie grasses, agricultural succession of soybean and feedlot corn. Ghost flora—toothed or hollow-throated—projecting auricles, pollen grains fossilized in sediment. Purple, blue, green, gold, straw, many-brown, black-voiced—plain to ungulate and glire.

orrido (from the Latin *horridus*, a derivative of *horrēre*, "to feel horror" (first half of the fourteenth century)): a rocky throat of tremendous depth and beauty, formed by the action of water falling through caverns and down ravines, making for tumultuous passage into an isolated valley. Under modernity, a corridor from which electrification for other, more economically generative valleys can be drained.

The Other: to talk about "the other" seems to predetermine violence against this other. Actually, the mere usage of the word "other" itself is a form of violence, even if it is used in a tolerant and accepting context. To acknowledge that differences exist *without* adhering or implying a whole or an identity: a skin color is merely different than another skin color, for example, or a genital is merely different than another genital. When "the other" is an impenetrable whole and not just mere differences, violence is possible: a person of color is formed by taking one—already constructed—feature and reducing a living breath to it. This is par excellence symbolic violence. An identity, final and rigid, hence, an "other," also and by necessity final and rigid. Relying on the category of "mere differences," in contrast, could help establish an ontologically flat surface where few points of attack/violence can present themselves.

phylogeny: coined by Ernst Haeckel (think drawings of diatoms, shells, jellyfish, spiders, etc.), 1866, to describe the organismal lineages we all passed through; phyla (φυλή, tribe, stem, race, branch) geny (born). Troubled by Haeckel's repugnant ideas of a hierarchy of "races." Wrest it from his hands and give it back to all the animals and plants—we all passed through roots and branches of the same tree, beginning somewhere with a few molecules combusting (as Darwin suspected, as genome data confirms). In the mid-sixties, Lynn Margulis pioneered "symbiogenesis": we came about not just through competition but through acts of symbiosis. We carry evidence of species merger in our cells, of species relation in almost every structure we daily rely upon. Lobefin fishes did protolungs, acorn worms might have done something like a heart, amphibians did shoulders, jellyfish saw first for us. If we let phyla be taken over by its bedmate phylla (leaves, petals, sprouts, sheaves, sheets of paper), we clear a mute space where we are all tangled in and leafing from the same roots. (If we take it further, to its homonymic neighbor, philo, we fall into love.)

resistance: to be rooted and unruly. To be integrated into locale circumstance so to dismantle monoliths. To challenge monolithic orders and defy language itself, to defy the ways of the castle. To deeply see is to seek the roots upwards, downwards, and sideways. To see which processes monoliths serve. To counter forgetting and root, to expand and recognize stories outside of the monolith. Working with both roots and methods of dispersal. To seek outside of usual patterns of perception by seeing the familiar in its multiple possibilities. To make against the production of unseeing.

shadow: even if I'm angry the cedar was cut down, part of restoring balance is my response. New ecology, collective mind, calls for expressions of growth. When a wood lily blooms, a chord sounds. I feel tremendous energy flow from beautiful earth, for the quantum is diaphanous, not dialectic, and permeated by starlight. Time, transformation, unifies. My anger at destroyed land provides a structure that's appropriate, so I also feel peace—two emotions, side-by-side, natural shadow. There's still a world of contrast, but in color, not black and white, and in change.

skirt: to lift up and away, to shirk, to walk outside or around a zone of responsibility or an imagined periphery of complicity. This describes the casual and everyday practice of imagining oneself as belonging to the outskirt, edge, or perimeter of an ecological disaster, both morally and physically. As observed in the act of kith lifting their saris and under-petticoats to walk around, beyond, past, or attempting to otherwise physically transcend symptoms of ecological disasters in urban contexts—oil seepage into ground-gutters, toxic wells, garbage mounds, human waste tributaries—in order to perform a moral transcendence of responsibility and codependence on urbanization, underfunding of municipal sanitation, informal or grey economies, and complicity with hazardous and substandard housing. As an everyday practice, skirting attempts to construct a cognitive map (see Fredric Jameson) in order to perceptually and imaginatively neuter one's own social alienation from the urban "barrage of immediacy," where the cause and effect of environmental policy, like a diesel-fueled high-octane ouroboros, shit and eat the simultaneous fragmentation and homogenization of urban space. Skirting is a daily practice—lifting yards of chiffon, cotton, silk, and rayon blends away from organic and man-made waste—that underpins (but does not underwrite) a "system of operational combination" (see Michel de Certeau) composing a culture of consumption. It pulls back, folds away, lifts up, and partitions any zone of contact between the disaster and the self.

un-personism: wherein the poetic subject is a site of total permeability, of radical interconnection with the human and nonhuman living world. Not so much a negation as a dilation of O'Hara's "Personism"—which famously proposes an eros of poetic abstraction that evokes "overtones of love without destroying love's life-giving vulgarity . . . while preventing love from distracting into feeling about the person." Un-personism proposes a more inclusive embrace, an eros that extends from within-species to cross-species to the planetary, with "all life-giving vulgarity" intact. Un-personism can be poetically manifested by many means, including a probing of one's position in time and space, in which the individual dissolves into the gene pool, the species into the ecosystem, and the ecosystem into a continuum of changing relationships and dependencies. At its most extreme, un-personism may extend out to the universe, where it attains a state of cosmic anonymity, a form of the ultimate communal. At another extreme, it conjures an image of a rock formation in which human fossil remains lie intermingled with evidence of mass plant and animal extinctions. It is this apparition of future ruin which compels the backward-facing angel of history to turn around and face her destiny as the angel of the Anthropocene.

washland refers to the specific laundering (as with money) of a city park located between the downtown business district and an impoverished community undergoing gentrification in Cincinnati, Ohio. *Washland* also refers to any cleansing (e.g., by oil—see Standing Rock, merely the most recent example of neocolonial betrayal of treaties between conqueror and conquered) of a land, a cleansing of its biological, geological, and/or marine forms of life in order to extract its non-living resources. The United States of America is merely one country that can also be called *washland*, but to the extent this cleansing—primarily ethnic—was never complete (Native Americans were not driven to extinction), "we" have a moral imperative to resist the totalization of bio-geo-ethno-cleansing however much such erasures have found revived inspiration in the imminent future.

watershed: at the confluence of two rivers, the Schuylkill and the Delaware, William Penn settled his city, 1682. Built on the southeastern edge of fertile Pennsylvania piedmont, Philadelphia tilts; its creeks and stormwater drain into the Delaware's great basin. From landscaped lawns to the Wissahickon to the Schuylkill, from city streets to the Tacony to the Delaware—all the water that falls and runs, works its way, if it can, south, to the Atlantic. Everything the water touches leaves traces that travel with it: lead, Chromium-6, Roundup, PFAs, mercury, benzene, sulfuric acid. Plastics and microplastics. Hormones, antidepressants, countless pharmaceuticals. Because the rivers flow through our bodies, too: raw river water, once treated and drinkable, enters us and exits as urine and other fluids that flow back into the Delaware after they too have been treated. The water holds on to everything treatment doesn't remove. Though land, city, bodies all shed water, water, that universal solvent, can't shed its own memory, can't help but tell us of all it has touched.

[**archive** Kimberly Alidio] [**azhigwa** Aja Couchois Duncan] [**earth** Jordan Abel] [**The Great Plaints** Brenda Sieczkowski] [**orrido** Jennifer Scappettone] [**The Other** Maged Zaher] [**phylogeny** Eleni Sikelianos] [**resistance** Hoa Nguyen] [**shadow** Mei-mei Berssenbrugge] [**skirt** Divya Victor] [**unpersonism** Evelyn Reilly] [**washland** Tyrone Williams] [**watershed** Brian Teare]

Forthcoming from Wesleyan University Press in fall 2018

Third Song of the Child Soldiers

Adrian Lurssen

Song for instruments and empty tents

We are telling the story of a cheetah elephant zebra and lion
They get nothing except the dust

They are fighting over who is strongest
You don't want to hear something like that

You can see the city from here, but you can't hear it or smell it
Across plains punctuated by circles, grass-ringed bald spots

A patchwork of troops and rebels covers every inch of earth
Each instrument cut to play just one note

*

Wire screen over cage to protect men from falling rocks
Black honey musky with sunlight and nectar

Bantu boys gagged for silence and
They laugh so hard they have nothing to hold each other up

Thin whispers of skirts and all minds focus on honey
You don't want to see something like that

We are reading a story about nothing except the dust
Each instrument cut to play just one note

*

Rocks are smashed and washed by hand
They are fighting over who is strongest

But how deep should you dig to maintain human success
We don't want to ask something like that

I am reading a story about thunder across plains punctuated by circles
I am living in my daughter's house

The thin whispers of skirts as boys trail their elders and
Each instrument cut to play just one note

*

Hunters descend with dripping combs
They laugh so hard they have to hold each other up

As boys trail their elders
They are fighting over who is strongest

They hide nothing except the dust
We don't want to know something like that

Thin whispers of skirts and rocks smashed by hand
Each instrument cut to play just one note

Notes on Third World Subtraction

Zaina Alsous

The difference between scarf and veiled
The difference between contract and caught
The difference between vaccinate and vacancy
The difference between invisible and interest
The difference between art and found
The difference between time and erosion
The difference between rupture and return
The difference between alphabet and finger
The difference between wet and irrigate
The difference between madness and mercy
The difference between judgment and cells
The difference between subject and witness
The difference between speculum and sex
The difference between heir and sterile
The difference between fountain and FEMA
The difference between land and landed
The difference between vital and vibrant
The difference between lung and blue
The difference between riot and rot
The difference between election and immolation
The difference between name and named
The difference between import and salt
The difference between border and route
The difference between body and bodies
in the water

Desertification

Amanda Hawkins

Something about a boy who dies
just after his fourth birthday, his brain ravaged
like land cleared of itself, trees
broken off and pulled like teeth,
like land left bare after such
intensive agriculture
nothing of what once lived could live
there again. Of course the difference is
the sweet boy died
and we could hold his lifeless
body in our arms, and he could cry
from confusion and fear
when the doctors strapped him down
that last time to begin
the tests. Of course the real
difference is he was a body not a place,
though, if you ask his mother she would say he was
his own landscape.

Poem with No Water at All

Kayleb Rae Candrilli

You don't even have to look to know this world smells of lava
and the ways in which we've burnt it. The argument against heat

is a scarecrow smoldering from the inside out. The fields
are locust wing–dry and there is little hope if you are listening

carefully to the wind. Most mornings, the day opens its mouth
to spit dust and half-hearted salutations. I do not blame the earth

for its general fatigue but rather embrace the lukewarm
air we walk through. I understand the cough that comes

after finishing a carton. The saddest thing about humans
and the earth is sometimes we smoke

                                    when we don't want to.
                                    Sometimes we let it all in.

Sand Fire (or The Pool, 2016)

Douglas Kearney

Chlorine & smoke lit our eyes
since it was we swam while fire made
a boxer's ear of sky—
   sweet, let go the side:
you'll be fine—you dove
      your violet ring from deepest cool—
          just *let me worry*—while my blood, karo
& slick guts: how it is now—
      know how far the burning by
      how small those first responders fly
      at soot-bruised afternoon's skin—
my guts crack slick knuckles,
metformin putting work in deep—
your hitch at "how'd it start?"—
        you know yellow weather lights the litter,
spattered oil, common saltwort—
    don't breathe outside for days—
         copters ring around & spill
to slow the flower—you goggle water & what "fire's gonna"
eat eat *sweet yes* o *though not ours this time* because
    —let me worry over burning, over
drowning, how this molasses blood loiters,
over how we go below that which *just happens*—
        hold your breath &
deeper deeper then, until you

daughter, come up clutching
what's under
—come back striking
what's above.

From *Some Words from 40-Some Days Before the Eclipse Translating Lorca's* Danza de la Muerte *by Writing It in Rice Flour Around 40 Wall Street . . .*

Sarah Passino

twenty-first day

today everyone smoking cigarettes
looks happy & full of life & like
when they walk by the halal grill

they dont see just piles & piles
of parts of bodies & i envy
the world & everyone sweet

& light who i watch in this bright
morning light wondering how
they know where they are

if they dont trace surface contradictions
track gaps if they only tail suffering
to understand suffering

oh i see it everywhere & in the animals
at home by the cumberland K & i lie
on sheets on the screened-in porch

listen to july crickets eat her moms
korean salads & she sits up
& says *some fucker keeps*

saying everywhere is the factory & we laugh
& laugh & then i looked down
the alley & saw an owl perched

on an old street light & suddenly knew
he was not me & he was not apart from me
that the factory is the factory yeah but

whats the rest of this

The Ghost of Jack London Reports the Post-Apocalypse

Brian Tierney

An unseen beast
deciding

if you're worth it
jerks its head, continues

the circle—its stalk-

gyre widens
to welcome more

distance, more

light. Like a camera
with its cap on

in the darkness even
thank god your gun

is blind

& fangless: *I hate you* it says
suddenly

woke all at once
to what it's done

in the name of the water-

levels rising meadows
you sit among

now: you & your companion
dog

by a fire—a dog's bark
by a fire & waves

behind him
where condos had been.

Aubade

Nam Le

The birds are gone. Soil
blooded to rustfruit, eyebright,
a vast intention heavy in the mackerel
grass, on the silent-screaming wire,
the concrete sky, the sun that slow bomb.
You are half my living now
the coming word, the deep and
bastard mind, making each darkness
felt, each day ordinal.
Every thrust of mine You met.
    God, that seeds the hydrogen, seed me.

Dear Future Child

Kyce Bello

The winter the oil
dipped in the barrels and the desert was gridded

for drills and all the new wars began

was like every other except we learned
to sing harmonies as the children slept

and now and then rain clattered the roof.

He found the notes we needed—
I held the melody lightly between my lips, lightly

as they say to do with questions
and other things that waver in our hands.

That was the year we waited for the river to fill its dry bed.

It came in a black rush
until we staunched it with thirst,

and on nights we didn't take down our instruments
I wrote a book of letters. Each one began

Dear Future Child.

I feel you flutter, unborn, from the apple boughs out back,
hear your voice, that third note,

in its long echo backward.

In the distance between us, invasive roses
make the back passage impassable—

Bars of small leaf and barb.

The letters always end with a bouquet of purple asters that wilt
before I can weave them into crowns.

I drive to the market for more flowers

wishing that driving was already banned
and remember that at night when we sing,

the moment our voices separate is the moment they become beautiful.

Elegy beginning in the shade of Aunt Mary's mulberry tree

Camille T. Dungy

A week before the woman whose tree
    that golden dog was tied to died, I watched
my daughter trust its limbs. She sat still a long time
beyond reach of a buzzing that seemed to begin
    on the walk & grow louder near the front door.
    Thanksgiving is a word we use most often
in conjunction with feeling full nearly to excess.
    I mean what I felt witnessing that ascension—
    an ascension made by nearly every other child
who's grown up, even a little, around that house—
    seeing her trust her body doing something
    other bodies had already done. I am,
I hope you understand, not talking about my daughter.
    I need to remember how focused Aunt Mary was
on watching her body climbing so fast & so high.
There was something graceful in that ascension.
    This, too, is a way to speak about thanksgiving.
Her legs, her heart, her vision worked like necessary
magic. Then stopped. I can still taste the cool buttery skin
    of her forehead—though it's weeks ago now
I last kissed her. "Apple of my eye" I want to say
she called me, because she made me—some of you
    understand this—feel so deeply loved.
    But I can't put words in her mouth. The truth

is she craved peaches all summer. Fruit from the tree
in her own yard wasn't anything anyone wanted
to eat. But the mulberry made for good climbing. Cast
cooling shade. The week after she died, it was some relief
to stop pacing circles whose circumferences
measured our grief in time to see that retriever
—leash wrapped at the place the trunk split.
She bounded & pranced in what we took to be wild
joy before we understood what truly moved her.
Lord. Oh, Lord. Please understand how much—
I think even now—the woman we loved loved
beautiful animals. What sense is there to make of this?
We watched that gorgeous creature run through the house
out to the other yard. She'd been released
from the lead that kept her tied to a suffering
that came down on her body as a mad hornet swarm.
No sense in this either, but as we watched her pass
we could have sworn she was still dancing.

Office of American Innovation

Elsbeth Pancrazi

They loved the earth they said

one does not shun earth here

with their different ways of showing it:

the first lady who with her limo window frames the silent park under snow

the birdwatcher who gets out into the center of the mudflats in that car
they lied about

the ledger of surveys, deeds, rights of way and easements

your neighbors with their come-hither lawns

and the poor who watch the storms closer than any person with insurance
could—

They said they were reserving the right to look at things from a philosophic-
geological perspective

That is, the people who suffer will suffer and if the universe does turn
out to be sentient

that won't be the thing that makes it cry—

They clarified their earlier statement

We never needed earth they said

    —but didn't you love it?

They said we never needed to love it

the unfaithful glaciers, temperamental atmosphere, fraught streams—

They say earth never loved us

I say *it hasn't lied to us yet*

Lovers in a Time of Nuclear Power

Mutsuo Takahashi

You, the ones I love, I love, I love
You, my lovers in an age of nuclear power
Beyond the window covered in black cloth
There is not a single tree to cast a shadow
Nor a single bird to wing through the air
Our field of vision is filled with thronging towers of flame
Invisible, infinitesimal gods that split and fissure continuously
Sealed in darkness, we are buck naked
There is no day, nor night, hundreds of times
No, thousands of times, we suck at one another
Ten thousand times, one hundred thousand times
We rub ourselves together
Now, no love juices overflow, no words of love leak
We discharge blood-water, painful itches run through our branches
The dead, dead, dead children born of our imaginary childbirth
Are covered in blood, for them we open the garbage in the corner of the room
We are reduced to skin and bones, our skeletons show through
Wrinkled sacks of skin merely holding dried-up organs
Our thin chests press against one another, our pelvises shudder without end
Other than one another's eye sockets which we seek out
We do not see, nor do we try to
All we have is one another, the partners we will love
Perhaps we are making love now, that is unclear
We suck at one another, we bite one another, we indulge ourselves
Until there is no *we*, nor *me*, nor *you*

In the world of light beyond the window covered in black cloth
There is no longer any earth nor stars, our field of vision
Is filled with forests of towers of our endless desire
That continue to multiply, that continue to spew out flame

—*Translated from the Japanese by Jeffrey Angles*

An Old Song, a Frog's Song

Benjamín Naka-Hasebe Kingsley

> There once was a giant kci-coqols, a bullfrog
> big as a hill. He made love to the Lake
> and Her children were born of land and water, many
> as the pebbles on Her hips, the waist of Her shoreline.
> Now, when the Lake is poisoned and Her spirit
> will cause people harm, Her children are the first
> to tell us. They are the first to die.
> —as remembered by a Clan Mother of the Onondaga Nation

Sing long   on America   as One
body   but many parts   of the Lake
says   great   grandmother

Sing long   on all the tribes   who were
who   drank from Her   once-blue lips
knelt   to wash   a child's hair
long black   to   long black
who are now *not*   but   a ghosted edge
mislaid names   Red   how many
of kci-coqols'   kin   must have drowned
in our carnage   bellied-up   Native in Her body
where white man's   hands   were washed
blood red   to lake blue then   white again
says   great   grandmother

Sing long   on how many more   deaths
a flood   of broken duck necks   still
gulp for one last   melody   Trees gorged
with yellow-bodied   canaries   choke
on the cancer   of men's   love
for coal for oil for the   glacier's   hot
melting   in the chandelier   of a whisky glass
says   great   grandmother

Sing long   on the price   of blood
of black   soil   of treasure
if men could   silo sunlight   peddle
its glisten above   Her blue   body
they would   oh they   would
says   great   grandmother

Listen   for the old   song
for   the shore   song
for   the frog   song. Listen
for   Her children's   one small song

Then   sing
with your   whole   body
    sing
for all   who are   to come
    sing
says   great   grandmother
    sing

Jordan Abel is author of *Injun*, *Un/inhabited*, and *The Place of Scraps*.

Kimberly Alidio, a VONA/Voices fellow, is author of *After projects the resound*.

Zaina Alsous is a daughter of the Palestinian diaspora and an abolitionist. Her chapbook *Lemon Effigies* is forthcoming from Anhinga Press.

Desirée Alvarez is a multidisciplinary artist whose first book, *Devil's Paintbrush*, won the 2015 May Sarton New Hampshire Poetry Award.

Kaveh Akbar is the author of *Calling a Wolf a Wolf* and *Portrait of the Alcoholic*. He teaches at Purdue University and is the founding editor of Divedapper.

Jeffrey Angles's most recent translation of is Orikuchi Shinobu's classic novel *The Book of the Dead*. He teaches at Western Michigan University.

Rae Armantrout's latest book, *Wobble*, is forthcoming from Wesleyan in the fall of 2018.

Kyce Bello's poems have appeared in *Kenyon Review Online*, *Anomaly*, and *Sonora Review*. She holds an MFA from the Institute of American Indian Arts.

Aase Berg is the author of seven books of poetry, most recently *Hackers*, published in English translation in 2017.

Mei-mei Berssenbrugge is author of twelve books, most recently, *Hello, The Roses*.

Kyle Booten, a fellow in the Neukom Institute for Computational Science at Dartmouth, has poems in *Fence*, *Western Humanities Review*, and *Poor Claudia*.

Jericho Brown is the author of *The New Testament* and *Please*.

Kayleb Rae Candrilli is author of *What Runs Over*. They serve as an assistant poetry editor for *BOAAT Press*.

Jesús Castillo was born in Ciudad Valles, México, and moved to California when he was eleven. An NEA Fellow, he is author of *Remains*.

Abigail Chabitnoy's debut collection, *How to Dress a Fish*, is forthcoming from Wesleyan University Press.

Adam Day is the author of *Model of a City in Civil War* and directs The Baltic Writing Residency in Sweden, Scotland, and Blackacre Nature Preserve.

Aja Couchois Duncan's *Restless Continent* won the 2017 California Book Award.

Camille T. Dungy's most recent books are *Trophic Cascade* and the essay collection *Guidebook to Relative Strangers: Journeys into Race, Motherhood, and History*.

Noah Dversdall studies English and Chinese at Kenyon College.

Gyrðir Elíasson is an Icelandic poet, translator, and recipient of the Nordic Council Literature Prize. He publishes nearly one book a year.

Tracy Fuad is an MFA candidate at Rutgers-Newark. Her chapbook, *Facts About Saddam Hussein*, is forthcoming in Spring 2018.

Johannes Göransson, author of *The Sugar Book*, has translated five books by Aase Berg. He teaches at the University of Notre Dame and edits Action Books.

Carolyn Guinzio's fifth collection, *Ozark Crows*, excerpted here, is forthcoming from Spuyten-Duyvil Press.

Amanda Hawkins holds a MATS from Regent College. Recent poetry can be found in *Tin House*, the *Missouri Review*, *Crab Orchard Review*, and *Orion*.

Sheikha Helawy was born in the Bedouin village of El-Roi, which was destroyed by the Israeli government. Her work has been translated into Hebrew, German, and French.

Claire Hero is the author of *Sing, Mongrel* and three chapbooks, most recently *Dollyland*.

Brenda Hillman teaches at Saint Mary's College. She is author of *Extra Hidden Life, among the Days* and a co-translator of Ana Cristina Cesar's *At Your Feet*.

Joan Naviyuk Kane is author of *Black Carbon*. She teaches in the low-res MFA program at the Institute of American Indian Arts, Santa Fe.

Douglas Kearney is author of *Buck Studies*, *Mess and Mess and*, and *Patter*.

Benjamín Naka-Hasebe Kingsley belongs to the Onondaga Nation. Recent work has appeared in *Best New Poets*, *Iowa Review*, *PANK*, and *PEN America*.

Nam Le currently lives in Melbourne, Australia.

Diana Keren Lee's work has appeared in *Denver Quarterly*, *Portland Review*, *wildness*, and *Prelude*.

Adrian Lurssen is originally from South Africa. His poetry has been published in *Fence*, *American Letters & Commentary*, and *Indiana Review*.

Matt Massaia is a poet, zine-maker, and musician. He is an MFA candidate in creative writing at Adelphi University, where he also teaches.

Irène Mathieu is a poet and pediatrician. A former Callaloo and Fulbright Fellow, she is the author of *orogeny* and *the galaxy of origins*.

Ted Mathys is the author of *Null Set* and two previous books of poetry. He teaches at Saint Louis University.

Meg Matich's first book-length translation from Icelandic is Magnús Sigurðsson's *Cold Moons*.

Christopher Nelson is the author of *Blue House* and *Capital City at Midnight*, and editor of *Under a Warm Green Linden*, which supports reforestation.

Hoa Nguyen is the author, most recently, of *Violet Energy Ingots*.

Kathy Nilsson is author of *The Infant Scholar*.

Greg Nissan is a poet, translator, and Fulbright recipient. His chapbook *Obstructed Views* is forthcoming from DoubleCross Press.

Elsbeth Pancrazi is the author of *Full Body Pleasure Suit*. She is working on a new book of poems starring the U.S. Secretary of the Interior.

Sarah Passino's work has recently appeared in *Broome Street Review*, *Poetry Daily*, *Underwater New York*, and *DIAGRAM*.

Rowan Ricardo Phillips is the author of *Heaven* and *The Ground* as well as the critical study *When Blackness Rhymes with Blackness*.

Yosefa Raz has published translations, poetry, and essays in *Entropy*, *Guernica*, *World Literature Today*, and *Jacket2*.

Marthe Reed's most recent book is *Nights Reading*; she is co-publisher of Black Radish Books.

Roger Reeves's first book, *King Me*, won the VCU's Larry Levis Reading Prize. His next book, *On Paradise*, is forthcoming from W.W. Norton.

Evelyn Reilly is the author of *Styrofoam*, *Apocalypso*, and the forthcoming *Echolocation*, all from Roof Books.

Emelia Reuterfors received her MFA from the University of Arizona. She lives in Kansas City and is an advocate for psychiatric and homeless populations.

Linda Russo is the author of three books of poetry and the collection of essays *To Think of Her Writing Awash in Light*.

Jennifer Scappettone is the author, most recently, of *The Republic of Exit 43*.

Brenda Sieczkowski is author of the forthcoming *Like Oysters Observing the Sun*.

Eleni Sikelianos is author of eight books of poetry and two hybrid memoirs.

Dennis James Sweeney's work has appeared in *Crazyhorse*, *Five Points*, and *Indiana Review*. He is earning a PhD in writing at the University of Denver.

Mutsuo Takahashi is one of Japan's most renowned living poets. His memoir, *Twelve Views from the Distance*, was translated by Jeffrey Angles.

Brian Teare is author, most recently, of *The Empty Form Goes All the Way to Heaven*.

Brian Tierney is a former Wallace Stegner Fellow at Stanford and holds an MFA from Bennington. He was included in *Narrative*'s "30 Below 30" in 2013.

Alissa Valles is the author of *Orphan Fire* and *Anastylosis*, a book-length poem published on thermal paper for the Whitechapel Art Gallery, London.

Divya Victor is author of *Kith*, *UNSUB*, and *Things to Do with Your Mouth*.

Nicole Walker is author of *Sustainability: A Love Story* and *A Survival Guide for Life in the Ruins*, both forthcoming.

Ellen Welcker is the author of *Ram Hands*, *The Botanical Garden*, and several chapbooks, including *The Pink Tablet*.

Tyrone Williams's most recent collections are *Adventures of Pi* and *Howell*.

Maged Zaher was born in Cairo. His collected poems appeared in 2017.